Bringing Paris Home

Bringing Paris Home

PENNY DRUE BAIRD

THE MONACELLI PRESS

For
Barbara D'Arcy and Paige Rense

And to my husband, Freddy,
who made the dream of living in Paris the reality

Published in the United States by the Monacelli Press,
a division of Random House, Inc., New York

The Monacelli Press and colophon are trademarks of Random House, Inc.

Library of Congress Cataloging-in-Publication Data
Baird, Penny Drue.
Bringing Paris home / Penny Drue Baird. -- 1st ed.
p. cm.
ISBN 978-1-58093-205-9 (hardcover)
1. Interior decoration--France. I. Title.
NK2049.A1B35 2008
747--dc22
2008013823

Printed and bound in China

109876543
Third Edition

Designed by Abigail Sturges

www.monacellipress.com

Contents

Introduction

An indescribable feeling greets us when we step into the streets of Paris. What is it about just being there that creates such a stir within us? All at once, we are surrounded by physical beauty and by ethereal stimuli—the smell of the streets, the sky, the street signs, the light. Can the air really be that different? Europe in general, and Paris in particular, fills us with a tingling feeling; our senses are constantly titillated. This heightened sensual experience stays with us throughout our visit. Can we bring it home?

When I was a young girl traveling to France and Europe the first few times, I had a physical reaction to being somewhere foreign. This strangeness or foreignness wore off over time; the feelings are so ingrained in me that they have become part of who I am.

In my late teens, European travel seemed exotic. My earliest memories of Paris include bus rides with my face pressed to the window. Hotels cost six dollars a night (no bathroom, of course) within the prevailing budget of Europe on ten dollars a day. Life was simple then: picnics of sausage under the Eiffel Tower; maps spread around with magic marker routes plotted out; never a worry about a hotel accommodation or good restaurant. One of my fondest memories is driving to Pont-Audemer, in Normandy, to have lunch at Auberge du Vieux Puits, reputedly the oldest inn in France, which survived a devastating World War II bombing that leveled the rest of the street. The Auberge du Vieux Puits was the quintessential French fantasy, with an incredible décor that immediately transported us into another century, if not another world, and sublime food—all this from a humble Michelin one star. Often these kinds of experiences cannot be repeated, but not so at this little inn. Over the years I went to Auberge du Vieux Puits countless times, and I always had that incredible rush, an incredible happiness, that alas, is impossible to replicate elsewhere. So amazing was the experience that I insisted that some Parisian friends drive two hours from Paris for Easter lunch. The husband, who simply could not bear that this petite américaine was telling him what to do, grumbled all the way. Many hours later, even he agreed that it was a special moment, a special day.

In my twenties, I made up my mind to spend every summer in France. I've been fortunate to have realized that goal. That decision taken, made with the hubris of youth, I also

made up my mind to learn French. I plunged ahead, registering at the Alliance Française in New York, where after two years and some struggle, I became a French speaker.

Each summer, I would settle in one region of France: the Dordogne, the Loire, Normandy, Brittany, and so on until I had covered the entire country. Each one is so different from the others, almost like mini-countries unto themselves, and each one influenced the decorator I have become. Every year I would get teary in August, the pull of responsibility calling me home while the tug and seductive powers of France held me in place. Several years ago, in the midst of one of my annual withdrawals, my thoughtful husband suggested we stay for the school year. Surprisingly enough I didn't say yes right away. But emotion ruled, and stay we did. We found an apartment that is completely typical by French standards and outrageous by American. There are fourteen-foot ceilings, eight fireplaces, each one worthy of a museum, and 150-year-old parquet floors.

Living in Paris presents an array of everyday chores made nicer by the surroundings, the choices, the attitude, and the idiosyncratic Parisian lifestyle. Parisians are greatly influenced by intangibles like the seasons. Food, wine, colors, habits all reflect seasonal differences. Parisians rarely leave their arrondissements. Each one supplies all they need—the *marché*, the *bistrot*, the café, the school, the doctor, and favorite stores are all there.

I live in an area filled with everything I enjoy. Steps away from my apartment are the Carré Rive Gauche (antique district), the Marché Bio (the cult-like organic market), my favorite café, Bar de la Croix Rouge, my favorite canteen, Le Voltaire, my favorite journal-writing nook, Ladurée, the Grande Epicerie (tantamount to buying groceries at Bergdorf's), and the venerated Poilâne, Gérard Mulot, and Barthélémy (bread, pastry, and cheese in that order).

I became an interior designer by happenstance. Trained in child psychology, I found myself doing interior design. I was influenced by Barbara D'Arcy's design book as well as by my parents and by friends already in the field. I dabbled with my own apartments, first in Chicago and later in New York, supplementing my instincts with courses at the New York School of Interior Design. As a young girl, I had watched as my parents decorated their home with the help of an interior designer. They chose Spanish-style furniture when all their friends chose faux French. The effect was chic and tasteful, so much so that when they moved some thirty years later, my friends couldn't wait to buy the furniture. The pieces I kept are chic and in style even today.

Bringing Paris home is not as simple as adding lace curtains or provincial pottery to your décor. It is something much more subtle and much more personal. It has to do with the philosophy of European living and many characteristics. To understand those characteristics, we need to take an exploratory stroll through the streets of Paris, eyes and ears open, to see what we observe . . . bringing home both the intangible as well as the tangible treasures that abound.

Architecture

*S*tep outside the door, glance around, and you know you are in Paris. The iconic images are known to all, even those who have never been there. Movies, art, photography, magazines, and literature paint a very clear, very real picture of the way Paris looks. Parisian architecture is distinctive, and it lives in our cognitive warehouse. The homogeneous "look" adds to the pleasure of being there. Even the simplest café is composed of elements that are repeated in countless other cafés. Monuments are carefully placed and seen in context, in the distance at the end of a garden, for example, or set off by a path. The low building heights, the permanent effect of the sky, whether gray or blue, the picture frame of greenery, the small parks all add to an architectural environment that defines Paris.

Architecture is a synthesis of many disciplines: science, mathematics, art, history, politics, and general aesthetics. Strictly speaking, architecture developed as the science of designing, planning, and supervising the construction of buildings for the most primitive cultures in which to live and worship. Around the world and throughout time, architectural design reflected the interests of the society it served. As early as the first century B.C., the Roman architect Vitruvius articulated the now-famous precept that architecture must incorporate *firmitas, utilitas, venustas*—durability, utility, and beauty. From the earliest times, architecture was seen not only as a means of creating shelter, but also as an important statement of beauty, something that defined its society and created a stage for living.

Civilizations are defined by their architecture, and therefore architecture opens a window into the past. Throughout the great upheavals in art and architecture, writers have extolled these three principles. Giants of architecture, whether in the fifteenth century, the nineteenth century or the twentieth century, all agree that proportion and practicality are essential but ornament and detail create the difference between "architecture" and "construction."

It stands to reason, then, that the character of a city or town is largely defined by its buildings, and this atmosphere is what residents experience every day. Even in medieval

times, the nature of the architecture affected how people felt and functioned. During this period, the architect, often also the builder, was generally anonymous. By the time of the Renaissance, architects were considered artists, and names such as Brunelleschi and Palladio became known. Buildings were thought of as "belonging" to an individual architect. To this day, the Duomo in Florence is known as "Brunelleschi's Dome."

Paris is, for the most part, a product of the late nineteenth century. In 1853 Baron Georges Haussmann was selected by Napoleon III to redefine the city of Paris, and he did so rapidly. He literally galloped through Paris, tearing down shanties and slums, draining marshes, and replacing narrow alleys with broad, beautiful boulevards and grand open spaces. He imposed a standard building height, and the new structures were similar in style and feel, all made of Oise limestone and articulated with magnificent ornamentation. Inside ceiling heights are colossal, and the floors, wonderful oak parquet, have lasted more than a century with nary a damage. The boulevards are lined with wide sidewalks, which protect cafés from the traffic. The planning was done with people and day-to-day living in mind. Trees line almost every boulevard, and small parks are found in every arrondissement. Other than the odd 1920s building and some other new construction interspersed here and there, the city has remained largely homogeneous in its architecture. Perhaps the greatest distinction between Paris and American cities is this homogeneity of style.

The aesthetic side of architecture is so important in France that interior designers are referred to as "*architectes de l'intérieur.*" Interior design should incorporate the same tenets as building architecture: soundness, function, and beauty. Principles such as proportion and volume are inherent in good design. In interior design, architectural features are just as important to the outcome as soft furnishings. Unfortunately, this aspect of design is often overlooked. If the goal is a European ambience, then appropriate architectural features should be introduced to create atmosphere.

Architectural features can be added to a room in many ways. Moldings, fireplaces, use of stone and reclaimed materials, columns, pilasters, woodwork, paneling and even paint can add architectural interest. Whether functional or decorative, fireplaces create a focal point and add an aesthetic element to a room. They can be simple or elaborate floor-to-ceiling affairs, and they can be adorned with a variety of accessories.

Moldings come in a myriad of shapes and sizes. They can be plaster or wood, both of which exist in an unlimited number of profiles. Virtually every effect can be achieved with molding, but it is best to avoid synthetic moldings, which tend to separate at the seams. The most common is the crown molding, or cornice, which is installed at the joint where the wall meets the ceiling. These can be quite sculptural or sleek and severe such as a "cove" molding. Cove molding, which is essentially an arc starting on the wall and reaching up to the ceiling, creates a fine effect in both traditional and modern settings. Sculpted moldings can be combined in layers extending up onto the ceiling. Classical sculpted moldings in plaster are so lovely that they are finding their way into modern settings that once would have been adorned with only a simple crown or even none at all. Today, it is considered chic to juxtapose walls and ceilings with opulent moldings and contemporary furniture.

Moldings can be applied directly to the wall to create an effect of wood paneling or classic *boiserie*. They can be painted in a variety of ways to further enhance their architectural quality. Baseboards can be high and dramatic and door casings can add another layer of intricate detail.

Moldings can be applied to ceilings to create a coffered effect where the pieces cross perpendicularly. This gives a strong feeling of depth to the room. Coffers can be embellished by a run of crown molding along the the inner edge, preferably the height of the coffer itself. Beams can be created out of plaster or added by installing authentic, reclaimed wooden beams. Plaster beams can be trimmed with crown molding, but reclaimed wood is best left in its natural state. Molding or panel treatment on doors creates architectural focal points.

Judiciously placed columns and pilasters give depth and sophistication to a room. Pilasters have the added advantage of concealing wiring for sconces. Columns and pilasters can be plain or fluted, simple or adorned with capitals and plinths.

Wood paneling, either in solid wood veneers or paint-grade wood, can yield outstanding results. In old Parisian homes, walls are often covered with paneling, or *boiserie*. The most elaborate period rooms have paneled walls; later, moldings in paint-grade wood were applied directly to the wall in patterns of rectangles of varying dimensions. Narrow, vertical rectangles topped with a horizontal molding, or a chair rail, are often applied to the lower portion of the wall. Above the chair rail, the wall can either be plain or divided into large rectangular panels. The panels are always designed in relation to the dimensions of the wall and its architectural features such as doorways. In classic French design, the walls and moldings are the same color, but occasionally these rectangles are filled with fabric or other materials. In the case of wood paneling, moldings are curved, or cut from the solid wood partner of the wood veneer, which serves as the background. Again, these moldings can be applied, but most often the paneling is a series of raised and or recessed panels, created by layering the wood pieces themselves. Paneling of this sort is topped by a crown molding as well, and there may be a chair rail or other ornamentation such as a volute, or corbel, pilasters, and other trim pieces. Bookcases often continue the paneled effect. Much of the paneling in grand buildings in Paris—stately homes, museums, palaces and the like—contains *boiserie* of the Louis XV and Louis XVI periods, with heavily sculpted motifs at the top of the rectangular panels. Although reproducing paneling can be costly and requires skilled cabinetmakers, it is still possible to find entire rooms of paneling for sale at reasonable prices in the Marché aux Puces and the French countryside. *Boiserie* fragments also exist, and rooms can be designed with them as well. Entire bed surrounds or niches created from fantastic walnuts and fruitwoods are sometimes available in the Puces.

Stone, especially the reclaimed variety, can add another architectural element. Whether on the floor of a room or on its walls, stone provides a room with incredible texture. Reclaimed stone can create a chateau-like feeling in a space. Stone elements such as lamps, vases, or urns, properly placed can also help with this mood.

The look and feel of a wooden Parisian floor was once almost impossible to achieve in the United States, but original *parquet de Versailles* floors are now available, and even an expert would agree that the floor once installed appears more than one hundred years old—because it is!

On the streets of Paris, visitors are surrounded by the architecture of an earlier time, the architecture of an epoch with great emphasis on beauty and on form over function. They are immersed in the values of another age, when life was less hurried, where beauty was expressed openly and constantly. These architectural features may not exist on the exteriors of the buildings we live in today, but they can certainly find their way into the interiors.

ABOVE
*Raised panels and pilasters accentuate
the double-height entrance foyer.*

OPPOSITE
*An eighteenth-century walnut bookcase adds
architectural interest to this library.*

OVEREAF
*This handsome living room incorporates an array
of French elements: a painted coffered ceiling;
an antique limestone fireplace and trumeau with
a display of country ceramics on the mantel;
overscaled wrought-iron lanterns; and architectural
elements used to support a glass tabletop.*

OPPOSITE

Wood paneling adds warmth and richness to this library.

ABOVE

A spiral staircase from the Marché aux Puces leads to a second-floor library.

A large, classic gallery is reinvented by creating a oval of floor to ceiling mahogany bookcases, complete with curved, book-clad doors.

Refinished original oak paneling evokes the atmosphere of an earlier era.

This family room is entirely clad in two-by-six inch wood siding, giving it a country look.

White plaster coffers and multiple ceiling beams give this room its definition.

Skylights and beams add to the overall architectural detailing of this poolroom. Limestone installed as raised paneling creates the effect of wainscoting.

LEFT
An entire wall of period walnut boiserie, a rare find, is combined with floral toile fabric to evoke a country chateau atmosphere.

BELOW
Vertical wood siding and reclaimed beams create a charrming country bedroom.

Two ways of using moldings to evoke different moods. On the left, clean lines and angular motifs create a formal effect; on the right, curved moldings and musical motifs give a fluid feeling to the boiserie.

Moldings make this ceiling unique.

A bed recessed in a niche is typically French. Here a painted screen, or paravent, *depicting the path of the sun through the day creates an architectural setting for the bed.*

Fireplaces

*F*ireplaces began as simple pits of fire inside primitive dwellings used for warmth and cooking. Until the sixteenth century, fireplaces followed the Saxon tradition: they were placed in the center of rooms with open hearths. When two-story buildings made this impractical, fireplaces were moved to outside walls and vented up the side of the building through a chimney. Over the succeeding centuries, there were a host of innovations all meant to make this central and only heating source more efficient. One innovation, credited to Prince Rupert of Bavaria, raised the fireplace grate to improve airflow. Benjamin Franklin invented the convection chamber, but the most successful improvement was Count Rumford's firebox. Tall and shallow, this design helped draw smoke out of the room or building and is still in use today. The fireplace eventually lost its heating role, but its secondary functions remained important. For centuries, families congregated around the fire for warmth, and the notion of the hearth as the center of the home has endured. This secondary function of fireplaces is symbolic; even without heat, fireplaces generate the idea of warmth and coziness.

From an architectural point of view, fireplaces are a physical presence. Whether traditional or modern, ceiling height or shorter, massive or diminutive, fireplaces add a strong architectural element to a room. In fact, the fireplace mantel often defines the architectural design of the room. This architectural element often relates to the center of the room, and other features—doors, windows, columns, and woodwork—are designed in relation to it.

European and French interiors are always designed with fireplaces. In a way, the fireplace is symbolic of generations of classical room interiors. In almost every case, hotel rooms in Paris will have one, as will every public room of the hotel. Similarly, the museums created from residences, the Louvre included, and all the historic buildings have fireplaces in every room. And so the fireplace becomes part of the feeling we know as French, the feeling we are trying to describe and quantify, the feeling we are trying to bring home.

When we speak of fireplaces in this way, we are referring to the fireplace mantel, or chimneypiece, rather than the fireplace opening, or *foyer*. The mantel gives the fireplace

its individuality, its flair, its decorative aspect, its seductiveness. Originally designed to "catch" smoke and protect from the hazards of fire, the mantel became the most artistic feature of the room. The mantel makes a strong statement in a room, not the least because of its sheer size. It can be extremely tall, even reaching to the ceiling. But more often, the mantel ends somewhere between one-third and two-thirds up the height of the wall. When the mantel reaches the ceiling, it is said to have a *trumeau*. This refers to an over-mantel, made either of the same stone as the mantel or a wood paneling. In the case of stone, the mantel is usually limestone, of a rustic nature and from the seventeenth or eighteenth century (or earlier). Mantels such as these are usually found in the country or have

been removed from old chateaux. When executed in wood, the *trumeau* is made of old paneling or *boiserie*, generally matching the rest of the room. Often the center of the panel is filled with mirror, but occasionally there is a painting. Since *boiserie trumeaux* were often part of the room decoration and not part of the mantel itself (usually marble), *trumeaux* are sold on their own in flea markets and antique stores. These over-mantels give a very dramatic and grand look to a room. While the size and weight of an all-stone mantel may seem daunting and must be properly evaluated for engineering purposes, large stone mantels are not prohibitively expensive to ship to the United States.

Mantels reflect different periods of French design. As with furniture and decorative arts, elements changed with the succession of kings (and queens). Since architecture and architectural detail predate furniture by hundreds of years, mantels were both a functional necessity and a major decorative statement. Limestone mantels were a simplified version of floor-to-ceiling stone mantels. Marble mantels were their more elegant cousins. Marble mantels always reflect the period in which the building was constructed, and it is possible to find them in every shade of marble imaginable and in styles that coordinate with furniture of the reigning monarch and transitional periods—Régence, Transition, Directoire, and Restauration.

Perhaps the most popular mantel designs come from the period of Louis XV in a style that has become known as rococo. These mantels are characterized by serpentine fronts, accentuated by fluid curves with the "S" and "C" forms. They are also marked by graceful and prominent *jambes*, or legs, ending either in a scroll, where the *jambe* meets the mantelshelf, or by corbels that seem to hold up the mantelshelf. These scrolls can be simple, but they often end with capitals reminiscent of Corinthian columns. Mantels from this period are carved with scallops, leaves, and shells. Ornate friezes with graceful garlands meet in the center, usually with a decorative motif, often a shell, or *coquille*. The graceful curves and the carved motifs epitomize Parisian ambience.

At the end of the eighteenth century, style and taste were greatly influenced by the ideas of ancient Greece. Today, a Louis XVI or Directoire mantel with its emphasis on classical Greek motifs and straight lines, can be incorporated in more contemporary, minimal settings with great success. Under Napoleon, winged eagles, laurel wreaths, and other regal, "victorious" motifs were incorporated in decorative arts including mantel design. Marbles began to be eclipsed by beautiful hardwoods and precious stones, such as malachite. This style—chic, sleek, and masculine—prevailed through much of the nineteenth century.

Today, the supply of French mantels spans more than three centuries of design and roughly twelve periods of French style. The mantel can be curved, fluid, and graceful or straight-lined, chic, and severe. It can be elegant and formal, or simple and earthy. A mantel can blend into the color scheme, either tone-on-tone or monochromatic, or match the color in a room with a strong color scheme. In a library with dark wooden paneling, one might opt for a rich jewel-toned mantel such as forest green or oxblood. Or one might choose to contrast with the color scheme and make a statement. A pale creamy living room might be greatly enhanced with a dark yellow or ochre mantel.

Mantels can be equally dramatic and attractive without an over-mantel, but the wall must be filled with another decorative element. Frequently, a mirror or painting is used. A mirror is often trimmed with a pair of sconces and surrounded by other moldings. With paintings, it is preferable not to use sconces, but a trim of molding can enhance the painting itself, creating a "frame" around the frame. Sometimes the space can be filled with an architectural element, such as a molding or *boiserie*, or architectural artifacts. In some cases, pairing a wooden *trumeau* with a marble mantel can create an interesting look.

The mantel itself presents an opportunity for even more atmosphere. Depending on its depth, a mantel shelf serves as a base for visual layering, achieved with objets of varying nature. Very often the centerpiece would be a clock, often flanked by a pair of *cassolettes* or *tazzas*. Together, this triad is called a *garniture*. Since the French mantel clock is often large, a *garniture* of this type will give the mantel a finished look. When a clock alone is the centerpiece, it is preferable to have a few strong architectural accessories rather than many small items. The exception to this would be a collection of some sort. Sets of antique bottles, globes, inkwells, candlesticks, can all look dramatic and charming when grouped together on a mantel. If sconces aren't hung above a mantel, then thin lamps or candelabra can balance a clock on either end of the mantel. Today, pairs of standing lamps, to the left and right of a fireplace, are in vogue, and they also provide an excellent source of lighting for the fireplace vignette itself.

Fireplace screens, andirons, firebacks, and fireplace tools complete the overall look. Screens can be metal, such as bronze (elegant and dressy) or wrought iron (rustic and earthy), or glass trimmed with metal. There are also summer screens, intended to cover the fireplace opening when the fireplace is not in use. These can be very glamorous affairs, usually wood framed tapestries or old French weavings. Andirons, which support the logs, are made in a variety of metals, frequently wrought-iron shafts with brass ornament or entirely brass. They can be massive, extending all the way to the top of the firebox, or diminutive and dainty. Fleur-de-lis and other royal insignia, balls, spokes, and cupped bowls are just some of the hundreds of decorative motifs on andirons. Fireplace tools should marry well with the andirons. It is becoming increasingly difficult to find complete sets of tools and even harder to find sets with their own stands. Tools can be tall or short, heavily embellished, or simple, in brass, iron or wrought iron, but care should be taken that all three or four pieces have the same handles. The taller the tools, the more dramatic the look, even if the large tools were meant for a larger fireplace in another era. The last element of a French fireplace ensemble is the fireback, a plaque that was affixed to the back of the *foyer*. Though not necessary in today's fireplace construction, these wrought-iron plaques, embellished with fleur-de-lis and crests add that "oh so French" flavor to the look of the fireplace.

ABOVE
A magnificent carved marble mantel is enhanced
with a rare gilded bronze fire screen and
accessorized with bronze tazzas and cassolettes.

LEFT
Pine paneling creates a country atmosphere in this
family room. The mantel, made from the same
pine, is accessorized in the French manner with
a Restauration period clock and matching tazzas.

PRECEDING PAGES
A Louis XVI white marble mantelpiece is sleek
but classic, adding a regal look to this sophisticated
living room.

PRECEDING PAGES
*A bold mantel design dominates this room and
gives it character.*

RIGHT
*A simple, limestone mantel and trumeau adds
height and charm to this country dining room.*

A Louis XV limestone mantel and trumeau works well even in the most formal setting.

Sometimes a simple, classic, wooden mantel works best, especially when the furniture is a mixture of different periods and styles.

An antique limestone fireplace, with trumeau, casts light and warmth into this pastoral setting. Since sconces cannot be attached to the trumeau itself, the same effect is achieved with two wrought-iron lamps.

A 1940s French mirror incorporating sconces
is paired with a classic marble mantel and a
traditional bronze garniture.

OPPOSITE
A pair of lamps lights the fireplace, a very
French technique.

ABOVE
*In a Bucks County farmhouse, the original fireplace
is dressed up with a leather fender and antique
French country pots, pans, and other ironwork.*

OPPOSITE
*Both the walnut paneling and the mantel were
designed especially for this library.*

Furniture

*T*he words "French furniture" are common parlance in the world of interior design, but often the term is only a vague concept applied to "country French," pieces marked by curved carving, usually in lightwoods, or fruitwoods. In reality, the definition of French furniture is far more complex.

French furniture has influenced design around the world since medieval times. Beginning in the seventeenth century, the taste of the court dominated all aspects of decoration and fashion, and the styles took the name of the monarch or ruler during each period from Louis XIII onward.

Furniture of the Louis XIV period, 1638 to 1715, is called baroque style, characterized by massive forms and sumptuous materials, carving and gilding. Ornate and expensive, these pieces were made almost exclusively for the aristocracy. Today, furniture of this *époque* is hard to find, very costly, and difficult to use.

The Regence (not to be confused with England's Regency at the beginning of the nineteenth century) was a thirty-year period after the death of Louis XIV when France was governed by a regent until Louis XV reached his majority. Regence furniture is considered transitional, not as extreme as Louis XIV or as excessively feminine as Louis XV; these pieces were the earliest to be designed on a more domestic scale and to incorporate oriental motifs.

Much more comfortable and sought after is the style of Louis XV. While still regal and ornately carved, furniture of this period was characterized by *cabriole* (shaped) legs and asymmetrical curves that also appear in paneling and other decorative elements. At the end of the eighteenth century, under Louis XVI, the rococo curves and asymmetry disappeared, and straight lines became the fashion. Carving was more apt to be geometric and classical. The furniture became smaller in scale and, therefore, seemed more feminine.

All these styles were adapted by artisans in the countryside and as they moved from Paris to the provinces, the forms and details became watered down. Thus, the tightly carved buffet or armoire in Paris (trimmed perhaps with bronze) became a loosely carved buffet

or armoire in Provence, with little or no bronze trim. Styles evolved based on the means of the buyers and on the skill of the local craftsmen. The availability of materials and local tastes also shaped these differences.

The first half of the nineteenth century encompassed a profusion of styles that corresponded to successive political upheavals. Most influential and recognizable is the Empire style of Napoleon, with its simple but solid forms executed in rich mahogany with gilded classical ornament. By the end of the century, both furniture and interior design were marked by the Victorian era, with its notoriously fussy and gloomy character.

The antidote was Art Nouveau. Suddenly design was not based on history nor was it an evolution of what preceded it. Instead, Art Nouveau took its inspiration from the world around it, without a backward glance. Art Nouveau emerged in Paris, with the designs of William Morris, Louis Comfort Tiffany, and others exhibited at the Maison de l'Art Nouveau, and soon spread to Berlin, Brussels, and London. As with many innovations, it was met with both awe and outrage; people either loved or loathed it.

Influenced by the rococo and by botanical symbolism, Art Nouveau is associated with elongated curves, flowers, leaves, buds and the like, the flowing forms of Raphaelesque women and their hair; a parallel expression relies on a whiplash line form, vertical lines, and exaggerated height. These two distinct looks are not always concordant, and fans might be attracted to one and not the other. These design features were executed in exotic woods, silver and glass, marquetry, and even semi-precious stones.

One of the most influential designers of both the Arts and Crafts and the Art Nouveau movements was Charles Rennie Mackintosh. He developed his own style, a mixture and contrast of right angles and floral designs, which became known as the Mackintosh Rose motif. Besides leaving his mark on architecture, he worked in interior design, textiles, and home furnishings. These designs quickly crossed the channel and influenced furniture and painting in France.

The posters of Alphonse Mucha have come to symbolize Art Nouveau in Paris. Born in what is now the Czech Republic, Mucha moved to Paris in 1887, as did many aspiring artists of his time, and became the quintessential starving artist. In 1894 he achieved instant success with the life-size poster of Sarah Bernhardt as Gismonda.

Art Nouveau enjoyed a brief revival in the 1960s. Short-lived as a decorative period, Art Nouveau provides particularly unique aspects to contemporary design. The secret of using Art Nouveau successfully in today's interiors is to mix it discreetly with other styles.

The next revolutionary modern movement was the style now known as Art Deco, which manifested itself in architecture and interior design and in virtually all of the decorative arts including jewelry, textiles, fashion, ceramics, metalwork, and furniture. The 1925 *Exposition Internationale des Arts Décoratifs et Industriels Modernes* in Paris celebrated living in the modern world, as society left World War I behind and looked to a future of endless possibilities. The exposition introduced a bright style, with many contrasts and curved lines to entertain the eye, with the intent to evoke happiness and to convey joy and celebration. Art Deco became the rage in France and swiftly crossed the Atlantic to the United States, where it also became immensely popular. The look was unique, fresh, and new, and the contrast with everything that came before was startling. Art Deco provided instant relief, a chance for people to express themselves as modern and without clutter. Art Deco emphasized bright, vivid colors, stark, clear geometric and cubic shapes, and dramatic contrasts—chrome and cobalt blue, or crystal and black.

One of the most influential furniture designers of the twentieth century was Emile-Jacques Ruhlmann. First influenced by the Arts and Crafts movement, he turned to Cubist and Egyptian sources for inspiration. In 1919, he created Ruhlmann and Laurent, an interior design firm that produced furniture, wallpaper, and lighting. Their products were the height of luxury, with furniture made in exotic woods and ivory. Ruhlmann's cabinetmakers were so meticulous that his pieces have often been compared to the finest eighteenth-century pieces and are still considered so today.

Jean-Michel Frank had an enormous influence on interior design in his time and does so to this day. His work incorporated textures and materials that were considered new and daring, such as straight-lined furniture, leather, lacquer, and vellum (used on walls). Shagreen, today considered a hot "new" material was used by Frank to make furniture and wall coverings. Shagreen made an appearance in the 1980s and is both stylish and coveted today. Frank is credited with the Parsons table (surely an interpretation of Art Deco), which was made famous again in the 1970s by the late Billy Baldwin.

At the same time that modern styles, free of historical references, emerged, mass production allowed furniture manufacturers to reproduce eighteenth and early nineteenth century pieces accurately and economically. These beautiful pieces are now antiques in their own right.

Thus defining "French furniture" is a complex task. Many styles and elements define French furniture and present a panoply of choices for the collector. Many of these can be successfully mixed together to add a French feeling. These styles have influenced the world of design and incorporating them in the home creates that *je ne sais quoi* (just can't put your finger on it) sense of French style.

Louis XVI sconces and chandelier and a classically French tête-a-tête are successfully combined with a Dutch cabinet, English tray table, and art of different periods.

OPPOSITE
A leather trunk and black painted furniture suggest the library of a gentlemen's club.

RIGHT
Oak pieces in an elegant setting create a casual chic.

Wood and alabaster are an exceptional combination on the candlestand.

Marble urns on a Louis XV marquetry console create a classic French look. The mirrored wall behind reflects sets of morocco-bound books.

Contemporary upholstery brings an Empire daybed up to date.

An antique carved wood panel, with sconces added, becomes an unusual headboard.

1930s French folding chairs and glass and bronze tables are used in a clean, updated Palm Beach setting.

Paint and
Wall Treatments

*T*he feeling of a Parisian room is the result of a combination of factors, not the least of which is color. In Paris, paint is a topic everyone loves, but successful use of paint can be elusive. The kind of paint to use, the type of finish, special techniques, and color selection can make the most seasoned designer's head spin!

In the grand *chateaux*, *hôtels particuliers*, and manor houses of France, paint plays an important role in room décor, one that goes hand in hand with woodwork. *Boiserie*, or woodwork, was commonly used as an architectural wall treatment. Often, today, the color scheme of a room, as defined by its fabrics, is set against the backdrop of wood, which may, in fact, be a painted finish. Walnut, in its many varieties, and sometimes oak, provide the background color to rooms in many French homes. Thus, the color palette is made up of fabric colors set against a color in the brown family. Often, the *boiserie* was painted in a variety of pale colors using stain, paint, or gouache, which were originally applied evenly. Over time, however, the color seeped into the grain of the wood and produced an effect that was more variegated, more striated, and less opaque. Painted *boiserie*, old and weathered, creates a romantic mood with its dull, glazed-looking finish. As *boiserie* became more and more expensive and panel moldings were applied to walls to simulate its look, paint was used to replicate the effect.

In American architecture, it is rare to find period examples of paneled rooms except in the "cottages" of Newport and the mansions of the Gilded Age. Even in Paris, wonderful dark *boiserie* walls are the exception. But a similar mood can be achieved by using dark paint as a backdrop to give a warm, rich look to the shell of the room. Faux-painting can simulate the grain of paneling, and walls are sometimes painted from the chair rail down to and including the baseboard to give the look of wainscoting.

Even without the advantage of true *boiserie*, a Parisian atmosphere can be achieved with paint. Choosing the interior finish for paint is a topic unto itself. Flat finishes present a very chic and matte look, which works nicely with both contemporary and traditional settings. Flat paint is easy to touch up and is splatter resistant, and it has a durable

XVe GRAND PRIX AUTOMOBILE

COMPTANT POUR LE
CHAMPIONNAT DU MONDE
DES CONDUCTEURS

MONACO

19 MAI 1957

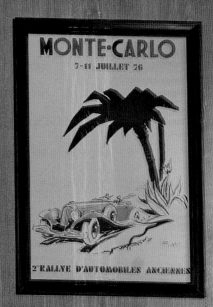

MONTE-CARLO

7-11 JUILLET 26

2^e RALLYE D'AUTOMOBILES ANCIENNES

low-luster finish, which cleans well with soap and water. Satin Impervo can take a beating and is great for covering imperfections. It is recommended for interior trim, doors, cabinets and wood that has been painted before. Semi-gloss and high-gloss produce a shiny finish. Semi-gloss is suitable and practical for doors and trim as is high-gloss. These finishes are also best suited to areas trying to make a statement. Glossy finishes should be applied over walls that have been carefully prepared (skim-coated or canvased) to keep imperfections to a minimum.

Paint colors should be selected after the overall palette of the room is determined. It is a mistake to paint a room a specific color, only to find nothing to match it, or that the subsequent choices no longer fit the original design concept. The fabric scheme will dictate the colors, which will enhance the décor.

The first decision is the choice between a dark or light backdrop for the room. Each has its advantages. Light rooms tend to be open and often help create a happy feeling. Dark rooms induce atmosphere and can seem cozy and clubby. Neither is right or wrong, and the ultimate goal must be considered in order to choose between a light and dark background.

When selecting a "white," remember that all whites are not equal. There are dozens of whites, each with its own cast. The best way to understand this is to look at a basic chart of white paint. It is instantly apparent that a white that just looks "white" when on the walls of a room is actually slightly yellow, pink, or beige. In fact, some of these whites can look quite dark when applied. In Paris, "white" means *blanc cassée*, which is actually "off-white." While this can also create a clean look, *blanc cassée* is less crisp than a true white. When using a white paint on the walls, use the same white on the ceiling. If the walls are not white, the ceiling white should have a very slight cast of the wall color. Ceilings are rarely painted a color unless a special treatment is envisioned.

Crown moldings should be painted the same color as the walls (as opposed to the color of the ceiling). This helps enhance the height of the room and is logical since the crown relates to the wall rather than to the ceiling. Moldings and trim (baseboards, window and door surrounds) should match the wall color. Do not paint the moldings or trim white unless the walls are white. White trim is passé and inconsistent with a Parisian look. If contrast is the goal, paint the trim a darker shade than the walls. It is rare in Parisian décor for moldings to be painted a different color from the walls. Real *boiserie* would be carved from wood of a consistent color, and applied panel moldings should follow that concept as closely as possible.

Decorative finishes vary widely, but they all seem to stem from traditional finishes from many different cultures. It is important to avoid trendy faux finishes, which become outdated quickly. Stick with the classics, which are bountiful in Parisian mansions. Paint techniques that are ages old, such as *strié,* simple glazed walls, and stucco, will always be in good taste. *Strié,* meaning striped, is a technique that consists of thin lines of paint in two tones of the same color. Glazed walls seem to have a film washed over them to create an old, worn, antiqued effect. Other paint finishes, such as sponging and other types of swirls, are strictly passé, and they are not reminiscent of French decorating.

Paint can play a more prominent role in a room than merely serving as wall covering and background. *Trompe l'oeil,* for example, is a major design and paint technique liberally utilized in French décor. *Trompe l'oeil* essentially means to trick the eye, from the words *tromper,* to trick, and *oeil,* eye. This technique creates realistic imagery and three-dimensional effects on ceilings, within coffers, on walls, as friezes, and in multiple ways on furnishings. It is not uncommon to see molding motifs painted around door casings or on

pilasters. Ribbon and reed, a classical design, is a typical motif in French décor. Murals are also seen in classic French design. In the same vein as real and faux *boiserie*, murals appear in place of tapestries. The elite classes of the Middle Ages hung tapestries on walls for warmth and for color. But tapestries were very expensive and often unattainable during the many periods of war and trade disruptions. Wallpaper was a practical way to produce a similar feeling. At first, these papers were hung like tapestries, but soon they were glued to the wall.

Wallpaper was very popular in England. In the middle of the eighteenth century the British Ambassador to France started a trend by wallpapering his residence in Paris with blue-flocked paper. Originally, tapestries told a story and murals continued this tradition. By the end of the eighteenth century, scenic wallpapers were *á la mode* (in fashion). Wallpapers continue to be extremely popular, providing a practical way to decorate walls.

The earliest paint designs were copied onto paper and then produced with color block printing. Thus the earliest *papiers-peints* were born. Eventually wallpaper became such an art that entire houses of wallpapers were founded. Murals painted on wallpaper and hung as removable panels were *de rigueur* in the finest homes. Today, several such houses still manufacture *papiers-peints* according to tradition. Zuber is one of the best known, with offices in Paris, New York, Los Angeles, London, and Dubai. Zuber specializes in intricate scenes depicting a variety of topics. These murals can be polychrome or *grisaille*, a version of pale monochromatic beiges or grays. Today, there are several other companies such as Merril which specialize in these papers. Although wallpaper murals are costly, they can be installed in such a way that they can be removed at a later time. Often these murals are installed above a chair rail, or dado, as was the tradition with all early wallpapers. Then, a solid paint color or another *trompe l'oeil* technique such as faux limestone or balusters can be utilized below the chair rail. Zuber, in fact, produces an entire line of designs that one can add below the chair rail. Wallpaper murals can also be inserted into panel moldings, which are then painted to match or complement the walls surrounding them.

In many homes in France, both historic and new, fabric is used in conjunction with paint as a wall treatment. Often rooms are upholstered with fabric installed over padding, from the chair rail to the crown. It is also common to upholster the area within the panel moldings. As with wallpaper scenes, the panel moldings match the wall color, which can be a light background color or a stronger color selected from the paper or fabric itself. Fabric can also be paper-backed and applied to give the illusion of upholstery without the work of the upholsterer. Fabric is also used liberally as bed surrounds, which are supported on wooden frames attached to the ceiling or wall. These crowns of sorts are liberally painted in a variety of subtle or not-so-subtle colors, often with gold leaf for accent.

As many French homes are richly embellished with architectural details, the use of paint and other wall treatments becomes an integral part of the décor as well as a feature that ties many aspects of the design together. In creating atmosphere, it is important to consider how and where to use the paint and other wall decorations and what kind of effect these will produce. Remember that with wall décor, as in many decorating categories, less is more.

LEFT
Rough-hewn antique chestnut strips create a frame for an intricate paint motif, a classic idea executed in a modern way.

OVERLEAF
A nineteenth-century tapestery is inset in upholstered walls.

"Jardin francaise" wallpaper by Zuber, a classical design classically installed. Trompe l'oeil wainscot paneling gives a dramatic sense of architectural detail.

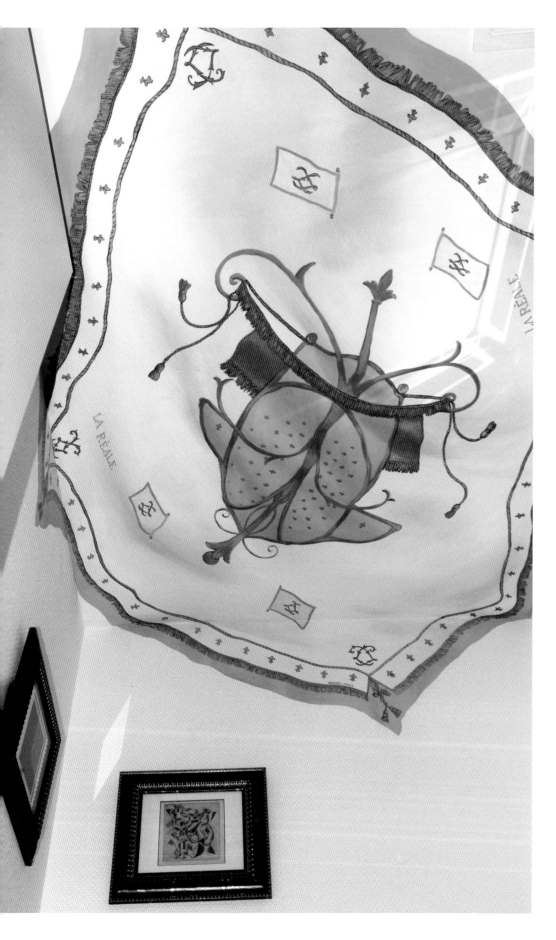

LEFT

A Hermès scarf painted in trompe l'oeil becomes a "canopy" in a powder room.

OPPOSITE

A built-in armoire acquires a character of its own when painted with an antiquing technique.

Multiple tones of blue and turquoise are used in these rooms. The walls are muted with brighter accents in the pillows and glass objects.

From coffered paper to faux fabric to real fabric wall upholstery, these treatments illustrate how important texture and detail are in completing a room.

*L*ighting is one of the most important elements that contribute to creating atmosphere in a home. In France, where much construction is extremely old, lighting is often added rather than planned in advance. Today lighting is typically coordinated with furniture layouts, but in the past, the placement of windows to admit natural light was the major consideration.

Interior lighting originally consisted of candle-lit wall sconces and chandeliers that could be installed without the constraints of wiring and switches. Weight posed no problem either; the buildings, constructed of massive stone and beams, could support anything. Although designed for practical purposes, candles and their gas-lamp cousins could not help but produce a romantic effect separate and apart from the original intent.

The discovery of electric light relegated candles to dining room candelabra for the most part. Today, however, candles have reestablished their importance in room décor. Considered one of the most romantic elements in a room, they can be found everywhere and to suit every budget. French women add candles to their décor as often as they use flowers. From the *de rigueur* Rigaud candle of the 1970s to the Dyptique candles of today, the French have always used candles liberally to create atmosphere of one kind or another. Lovely candle shops in Paris now offer an astonishing array of themed candles. For example, the popular Point à la Ligne store offers candles for every season. Candles range from fall harvest colors in designs such as grapes, vegetables and other vegetation to wintry sparkly white and silver concoctions of snow, stars and other motifs for the holiday season. For a "Rich and Famous" dinner for the New York Public Library, I covered the tables with golden castles, whose turrets flamed while golden coin candles shone brightly around them. In spring, green foliage is topped with beautiful spring flowers such as irises and roses. A clever and practical design aspect is that the floral portion can be replaced on the top of the candle's foliage stand. These groupings are very sophisticated, with entire gardens of hedges designed to evoke the architectural gardens of Paris. It is not surprising that

French women are charmed by the infinite possibilities that these original candles offer.

Although electric light does not provide the same charm, there are many ways that practical lighting can enhance the atmosphere in a room. Lighting can add drama, coziness, or functionality, and is a crucial element in creating comfort. Lighting can also help camouflage flaws and make the room feel larger or smaller.

Most lighting plans are conceived with ceiling lighting, either chandeliers or flush-mounted fixtures, as the main source of ambient, or overall light. Chandeliers are found in all classic French interiors. The variety of styles, sizes, and shapes is useful in filling hard irregular spaces since much commercially available lighting exists only in standard sizes.

Sometimes, multiple flush-mounts or recessed lights (down lights or high hats) are scattered in a pattern on the ceiling. Since recessed lights are generally found only in new construction in France, they are not part of the French lighting ambience.

Ceiling lighting should be the base layer of lighting, with each subsequent layer adding a dramatic effect to the room. Ceiling lighting can be harsh, and it is often improperly implemented, with too many bulbs and too much wattage, a problem that can be solved by installing dimmers. Sconces are often used in conjunction with overhead lighting since, depending on the size of a room, a single ceiling fixture may not provide enough light. If the room is very large, the chandelier will light the center of the room, but the perimeter will be in shadow. This happens in dining rooms and entrance foyers, rooms where there are rarely table lamps. In this case, it can be helpful and attractive to light the perimeter with sconces.

Sconces can take almost any shape and form in almost any material ranging from bronze, wrought iron, with or without crystals, globes, or even just as lampshades, with a hidden bulb. Although sconces are typically associated with traditional design, there are so many styles available now that even the most contemporary setting can be enhanced with wall sconces.

Placement of sconces varies with the individual requirements of the room and wall where they will be installed. In traditional settings, such as Parisian *boiserie*-lined walls, it is common to install sconces within raised panels or applied molding designs. In fact, in new construction, the paneling itself can be designed in relation to the lighting placement. Panel molding or other woodwork is usually designed with the furniture floor plan in mind and sconces follow, typically located in relation to the furniture placement.

In a living room, sconces may be placed above a sofa or on pilasters, stanchions, or columns that surround the room, establishing a regular pattern of light. In libraries, swing arm sconces are often installed above a sofa and to provide good reading light. Even swing arm lights, generally considered to be a rather recent creation, take on a different feeling when designed with a French touch. Today, it is considered quite chic to have small sconces everywhere with bronze or other metal shades or fabric shades trimmed in metal. These often take an Edison bulb (as opposed to candelabra bulbs) and the shade, which cuts the glare, adds another attractive, decorative feature. Lighting can be enhanced in libraries by adding sconces on bookcases. These can be applied directly to the pilasters, which serve as vertical separators. The other option is to install wall fixtures whose light shines down onto the bookcase itself. Dining rooms can be beautifully enhanced with sconces. Whether placed around the room at regular intervals, or above a buffet or on either side of a china cabinet, sconces add eye-level light in a room otherwise lit from above.

Wall sconces can also solve lighting challenges, such as dining rooms with low ceiling heights. In this case, low-voltage recessed lights in the ceiling can be combined with a series of sconces around the room. Corridors and small spaces can be difficult to light.

If the ceilings are low, try to install sconces at a higher level than usual, especially if the corridor feels narrow. This requires something other than a classic sconce design—something round that does not protrude from the wall or a sconce that is just a shade can work in this situation.

Sconces are also useful in bathrooms, often on either side of a mirror. Their finish should always match the hardware in the room and they can range from a standard sconce in a simple classic form, to the most ornate crystal and bronze Louis XV motif. Don't be afraid to be a bit creative here; a long narrow lampshade with three bulbs hidden within can be a decorative and chic solution for over vanity lighting, for example.

Many Parisian rooms are lit entirely by lamps. Often oversized, with huge shades, the lamps themselves become a decorative feature. They are often made from interesting *objets* and artifacts and therefore the sizes are commonly mismatched and quite unusual. If the base is a stone relic or an architectural element and therefore difficult to drill through, the cord may originate at the base of the bulb socket. Although this is impractical, lamps are wired this way even

though there are now other options. Almost anything can be wired as a lamp, and flea markets provide a trove of objects that can give special look to a room. In France, even standing lamps are unique, artfully made of columns and pieces of old ironwork. Sometimes very tall or quite short, they cast light at varying heights, adding to the atmosphere of the room.

Lighting fixtures in all shapes and sizes can be found, both new and old, in Paris. The Marché aux Puces is overflowing with unusual lighting, both in style and size. Lighting can be found from almost any period and can be made from a wide variety of objects to add an unusual French touch to your home.

OPPOSITE
*A vast Murano chandelier adds
dramatic simplicity to the double-
height living room.*

RIGHT
*Galleon sconces add a whimsical
note to this library.*

Sconces, table lamps, and standing lamps combine to light this living room.

OPPOSITE
A 1940s chandelier is an exotic contrast to the sconces between the windows.

RIGHT
An Ottoman chandelier—elegant and funky.

*Using four lanterns solved the problem
of evenly lighting this square room.*

OPPOSITE AND OVERLEAF:
Wrought-iron chandeliers enhance country kitchens.

ABOVE
A delicate chandelier works well with the floral prints
and the mouldings on this dining room door.

LEFT

A simple iron lantern is a foil to the visual richness of the fabric patterns.

OPPOSITE

A mirrored chandelier attributed to Baguès, well-known in the mid-twentieth century for whimsical floral crystals.

The quatrafoil motif of the sconces is also found in the shape of the lantern.

OPPOSITE

A wooden Regency chandelier is elegant and sedate but "dressed" with Hermès lampshades.

OPPOSITE

A late-nineteenth-century French crystal chandelier with three tiers and a twisted rope arm design is opulent yet tailorerd.

RIGHT

The wonderful symmetry of this dining room is enhanced by a pair of nineteenth-century French gilt metal chandeliers with crystals.

LEFT
*A chandelier covered in passmenterie,
a very unusual treatment.*

OPPOSITE
*An eclectic combination of fixtures:
A Louis XVI bouillotte lamp on the
desk, proto art nouveau sconces, and a
traditional chandelier.*

An antique billiards lamp and rough-hewn beams add character to this dining room.

Cafés and Tabletops

he Eiffel Tower notwithstanding, cafés define Paris and Parisians. Flapping awnings, charming colorful woven chairs, waiters in their long white aprons, and settings on tree-lined streets all conjure an image of a welcoming place to wile away stolen moments.

Although first introduced from the East to Italy, coffee has long been associated with France. Louis XIV, lover of all luxury and innovation, was mad for coffee. Having been given a coffee plant by the Dutch, he sent his naval officers to Martinique and to islands in the Indian Ocean to plant coffee. It is said (but hard to believe) that 90 percent of the world's coffee started from one of his plants. The earliest vendors in Paris were Armenians who wore oriental garb with long white aprons (still in evidence today) as they strolled through the Left Bank hawking their coffee. Residents leaned out their windows to summon them to their apartments. The coffee men mounted the stairs and brewed and served the coffee. A greater luxury is hardly imaginable. In the late 1600s, one of the colorful local vendors opened a little shop, or café, called Le Procope in the 6th arrondissement. It is still standing today on the rue de l'Ancienne Comédie. Cafés then began to proliferate all over Paris. By the end of the eighteenth century, there were 1800; in 1915, it was estimated that there were more than 350,000 cafés.

Cafés were, and are, essentially a microcosm of Parisian life. Everything from political decisions to social relationships passed through the café. People went to cafés to see and be seen. Left Bank cafés are famous for their literary associations. Cafés became a symbol of the artistic life of the Latin Quarter, Montparnasse and Montmartre. Cafés proliferated because they provided a place for people to mix and mingle and because they were at once inexpensive and accessible. Even today, patrons can linger endlessly over just one tiny cup of coffee.

During the Haussmannian period, cafés were a thriving mecca for journalists, writers, and artists. In the twentieth century, the legends Sartre and de Beauvoir made Left Bank cafés renowned. Resistance fighters plotted there, lovers escaped there, and cafés helped Parisians in general take their minds off the turbulent times. Today, cafés still strive

to provide the warmth, nourishment, and intellectual stimulation that made them famous. The Café de Flore, on Boulevard St. Germain, still has monthly "philosophy" evenings on its second floor.

Cafés have much in common, but they retain their individuality, both in style and philosophy. Each one has a pride of décor, whether chic or grunge. The décor itself is quintessentially French. The iron bistro tables, the resin chairs, woven in two colors on bamboo frames, the tiny cups and saucers in sturdy porcelain are all elements that translate well into a residential setting.

Just as the style of porcelain, glassware, and cutlery of the café reflected its daily use so did the tableware of the *bourgeoisie*, or wealthy merchants. In fact, all things Parisian seem to be related in one way or another to dining and cuisine. France is a leader in what is known as *arts de la table*. Roughly translated as "the art of the table," the phrase refers to all that is encompassed in table setting. The notion of *arts de la table*, like all elements of French taste and style, is taken very seriously. Dining is considered an event. The *bourgeoisie* enjoyed a social life centered around, among other things, the table. Even today many families gather at a large table on Sundays for a long, leisurely lunch.

As France became a leader in the design and manufacture of luxury goods, the tables of the bourgeoisie became more and more elegant and intricate. Louis XIV is credited as the founder of many of the manufacturers of important luxury goods. He banned the import of porcelain and ordered that factories be built in France. The Cristalleries de St. Louis and other companies—Baccarat, Bernardaud, Raynaud, Haviland, Christofle, Puiforcat among them—have been producing the finest china and crystal for three centuries.

In France, in restaurants and private dining rooms, careful attention is given to table accessories. This is true, whether the setting is casual or elegant, which explains why visitors to France can be equally impressed with a setting in a café or in a grand restaurant. It would be so simple if it were just a matter of using nice china and crystal, but, as with everything extraordinary, there is more to it than that. French hostesses incorporate a variety of "props" in their table design. Whether embellished with flowers or figurines, tiny dishes filled with nuts or candies, *objets* of any type, the table piques our senses.

The look always starts with the overall setting, the dining room itself. As with all decorating, proportion is of utmost importance. There were once many rules about how a table should be dressed, but today these have been relaxed. It is classic to use china of all the same pattern, but more and more often sets are mixed together. In this case, different components of the table setting are coordinated by mood and color. In France it is customary, but not mandatory, to use tablecloths, most often in classic white. Napkins are oversized and often heirlooms. The matched set is not as common.

There is often something unexpected in a French table setting. Dinner plates were originally small, but the trend to oversized has taken hold. Small, assorted dishes, for example, the pickle dish, are frequently incorporated in the setting. Serving dishes often have confusing or surprising names. For example, there is the "cake" dish. This is a misnomer of sorts. In French, "cake" pronounced as in English, is a small loaf cake, as we would call pound cake or banana loaf. Thus the "cake plate" is a long rectangular shape used for loaf cakes such as lemon or the fantastic *quatre-quart*. A round cake, as in a birthday cake, is called a *gâteau* and the plate is referred to as a *plat à gâteau*.

In creating a French table at home, it is important to consider everyday needs as well as special occasions. Once those practicalities are taken care of, it is the overall effect that gives the sense of the "loveliness" of Paris. The Parisian or French table is very coordinated. It is stylized in the sense that it is a vignette. The coordination includes the cloth or placemats, *set de table*, the china, crystal, flatware, and flowers or accessories depending on the occasion. Color and texture should be taken into account when mixing these elements. It is not necessary to use pottery and Biot glasses to give the look of the French provinces. A provincial print cloth can provide that backdrop for your own tableware, for example. For a more elegant setting, tableware can be enhanced with something interesting between each place setting—as simple as a nosegay in a silver timbale, or as elaborate as miniature porcelains. Guests are always appreciative of these efforts, and it is not uncommon for the guests at a Parisian dinner to give a hearty "Bravo" to the hostess.

In Paris, the emphasis is never on quantity but on quality. In the most lavish homes, there is just one set of china, often one that has been handed down from generation to generation. When entertaining, there is no buffet of desserts; there is just one, simply but elegantly prepared, and of course, delicious. The rule is to choose carefully and choose the best, then keep the rest simple but strive for perfection. The French seem to be able to do this effortlessly, the culmination of generations of training, it seems.

ABOVE
*Crystal and ormolu add sparkle to this elegant
dining room.*

OPPOSITE
*A walk-in wine cellar is the focal point of an
oenophile's dining room.*

ABOVE
Iron urns from the Marché aux Puces add a casual but elegant element to this table.

OPPOSITE
A dining table of mahogany and bois doré is pained with Régence-style chairs. Walls are lacquered and buffed to a high sheen and three Japanese painted screens hang as scrolls.

A classical epergne of flowers is surrounded by individual nosegays to embellish the depth of a round dining table. Sumptuous china and crystal by Bernadaud stands up to the strongly colored room.

An epergne laden with fruit, nuts, and sweetmeats conjures up an eighteenth-century banquet.

Convivial informal seating areas using café chairs and tables, glasses by William Yeoward, china by Zero One One. Napkins are simple, large, and linen, and typical of Paris. Woven Resen café chairs are infinitely practical.

OPPOSITE

Spring flowers—lilacs and hyacinths—complement the blues of the china and glasses.

RIGHT

The tall epergne here makes an architectural triangle within the pair of chandeliers. The china is Haviland, fabricated in Limoges. The crystal glasses were collected on various trips to France.

OPPOSITE
Classic choices from the Marché aux Puces:
a wrought-iron chandelier with a clock face,
bistrot chairs, and a wrought-iron table base.

RIGHT
European porcelain, linens, and silver
coordinated in blue.

❖ 163

MARC
PAUL

MARCHÉ
SERPETTE

Flea Markets

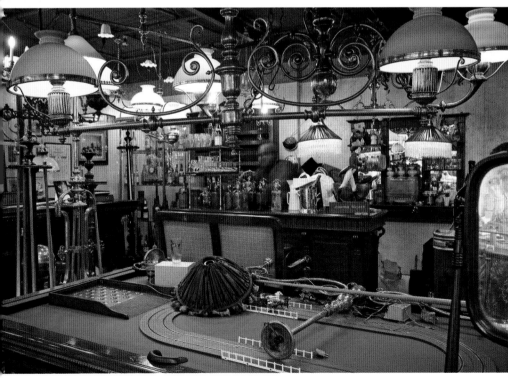

here have always been possessions that one person no longer wanted and another coveted. This is the most basic explanation for the origin of "flea markets" as we know them. In medieval times, vagabonds collected discards and resold them by placing their finds around themselves on the ground while others looked on and made offers. In the fourteenth century, this "profession" began to take shape, with its own set of customs and rules. At first, this was a completely unregulated, sleazy business, with vagabonds selling anything they could for any price they could get in any place and at any time of the day or night. Much later, perhaps at the beginning of the nineteenth century, merchants were required to describe their wares in writing and subsequently they were given plaques with numbers, a sort of license to identify them as permitted to engage in this trade. In the mid-nineteenth century, after Parisian authorities prohibited sales between midnight and six a.m., these merchants began to move their stomping grounds just outside the city limits. Thus, the markets at St. Ouen, Vanves, and Montreuil began.

Today's flea markets are vastly different from their humble origins. Marché aux puces is the generic term for flea market, and it applies to both the smaller markets in Paris, such as Marché Vavin, and the well-known group of markets in St. Ouen at Porte de Clignancourt, the metro stop on the northern edge of Paris. This is a microcosm of a village replete with "neighborhoods," each with its own flavor. Today, there are an estimated 2,500 merchants set up along fifteen kilometers of alleys in what is largest flea market in Paris.

From the top of rue des Rosiers, the view down the street reveals a myriad of shops, stands, stalls, and signs indicating the names of the individual sub-markets, each with its own specialties and loyal clientele. It would be impossible to absorb it all in one day, and

that should not be the goal in any case. The first trip should be an orientation to understand where to concentrate and how to define your interests. For many Parisians, strolling through the Puces is a Sunday activity all to itself; purchasing is entirely beside the point. For others, the art of collecting, trading, and arguing is the hobby itself, not necessarily resulting in any purchase. It is a more American idea to go to the Puces with a specific goal of buying something.

The more I go to the Puces the more fascinated I am, the more entrenched, the more aware of the subtleties of the life and the market, playing out behind the scenes. In fact, the Puces is much like a soap opera. With the same faces and characters, the same locales, the same personalities, the drama just stops and picks up again on the next trip, even if those visits are years apart. As is true of Paris in general, there is very little change. The fellow with the picture frames is still in his spot, as is the one with the bars. It's predictable and comforting. The Puces is a microcosm of Parisian life; priorities are obvious, and the role of commerce is noticeably different from that in an American market. Anyone will tell you about the reluctance of a vendor to stand up from his makeshift lunch when customers enter his stand, wondering if it's better to finish the meal or make a sale. First, he (or she) will size them up, trying to figure out if they are buyers or lookers. But, in fact, he will try to make the sale, and what comes next can be the most charming of interludes.

The rue des Rosiers is replete with individual shops as well. There are charming fireplace shops, and shops with reclaimed architectural ornaments. There are 1930s specialists with mirrored furniture, so popular today, to be had for a fraction of the cost of reproductions. And then there are the side streets, each representing a different "market" with its own type of merchandise and clientele. The Marché Serpette, located halfway

down the rue des Rosiers, defines the main section of the Puces. Serpette is a covered outdoor market, making it a bit fresher in summer and absolutely freezing in winter. So freezing in fact, that vendors and buyers, myself included, have taken to carrying little velvet boxes filled with hot carbon inside their gloves. (American glove warmers can work as well, but are less romantic!) Covered, it is dark, but it is also protected from the rain and elements. Serpette consists of a grid of alleys and cross alleys and can take an hour or three to traverse. In the center is a café, with surprisingly good snacks. After a few visits, you will know what to expect to find and where to find it.

Allée 1 has some of the best merchandise Serpette has to offer. Remember, this is not museum quality furniture. These are reasonably priced, decorative pieces, almost all of which have been repaired, even if the trained eye cannot see it. Novice clients at the Puces tend to find the merchandise expensive, but this is invariably because they have not priced it out at home. Nor does the euro/dollar inequity matter much. Whether you pay with expensive euros at the Puces, or in dollars at home, you will save money at the Puces. As you stroll down Allée 1, you will see many lovely things; perhaps what you are looking for, perhaps not. If you see something you like, don't hesitate to ask about it, whether you are hoping to purchase it or not. Vendors, in varying levels of English, love to discuss their finds, much as bread dealers in France like to discuss your menu before selling you a loaf of bread. This just takes a bit of friendliness on your part and an outgoing nature. It is important to greet the vendor before inquiring about a price. One always says, "Bonjour, Monsieur," "Bonjour, Madame," before asking the question. And don't leave out the monsieur or madame—a simple "Bonjour" is not enough. The vendor will always describe the item before giving you the price. The discussion and, perhaps, the negotiation to follow are part of the process, part of the moment, part of the fun.

Serpette is known for large furniture, but there is a variety of specialists as well. If you are looking for a vintage or antique-style bar, there is a dealer specializing in them. If you are after old Vuitton trunks to use as side tables or end tables, there is a specialist, or two. Many clients like the selection of 1930s and 1940s furniture that is available. Leather chesterfields are especially well represented—there is a vendor with dozens of them in an annex down the road. Serpette is a treasure trove of lovely and unusual lighting. Often you can negotiate rewiring for the United States as part of the purchase price. There are also chests, armoires, side tables, and club chairs. Styles range from a few seventeenth-century pieces through all three eighteenth-century Louis styles to prewar jewels of the 1930s and 40s and mid-century pieces in vogue today.

Behind Serpette is the Marché Paul-Bert. This market is not as well defined geographically, but it hovers around the back and side of Serpette. It is an outdoor market, freezing in winter, torrid in summer. A good pair of sunglasses is a must, as the sometimes-blinding light makes the objects hard to see. Paul-Bert is considered more of a *brocante*—not exactly antiques, but old stuff. That isn't to say that one can't find a gem or other very useful items, such as garden furniture. I'll never forget spying two red tortoise boxes in excellent condition, only to find that they were already sold. I've been looking for those boxes ever since. I never skip going to Paul-Bert. While I seem to buy less and less there, the memory of those boxes spurs me on. Here one can find lovely painted furniture, wrought iron chairs and tables, French bamboo, and kitchen decorations (useable and not).

Farther down the rue des Rosiers is the Marché Biron, a market with a split personality. That is to say, it has two sides, with entirely different types of merchandise and clientele. The covered allée is dark and dank and is generally similar to the Marché Serpette. The outdoor allée is wide and grandiose with furniture to match. This allée is perfect if you're looking for a chandelier for a hotel lobby!

The covered part of Marché Biron makes you feel as though you've stepped into another century. Although the stands are quite small, they are jammed with all types of furnishings. This part of Biron is known for armoires, chests (commodes), and small tables, as well as architectural elements, such as staircases. On more than one occasion, I have purchased complete circular staircases and had them installed in homes of clients. The *mise-en-scène* and its players are right out of Central Casting. People huddle together when it's cold, sharing a copious lunch of wine, cheese and bread. It's almost an embarrassment to interrupt them. Besides serious furniture, Biron often has its share of whimsical items—a huge pair of urns or a wall-hung fountain, for example.

The open side of Marché Biron is another matter. Las Vegas has nothing on the Marché Biron. The merchandise is on a greater scale and the booths are larger to accomodate it. This side of Biron tends to be filled with more formal furniture and lighting. Biron also has specialists in posters, glassware, silver and pottery.

All these stands, shops, and dealers have courtesy in common, a way of dealing that is honest, and mostly elegant. If you say it's sold, it's sold. A dealer would never sell it to someone later in the day if he were offered more money. When I was a beginner in the world of the Puces, I spied a "must-have." I was rushing to make a plane, but the vendor, who didn't know me, told me to take it and mail him a check. Since it is common to not

pay for merchandise on the spot, this type of trust works both ways. You've told the vendor it's sold and you will pay for it; he's told you it's yours and he will save it for you. I once paid for a chandelier from a vendor I hardly ever visit and promptly forgot about it. Two years later the vendor stopped me in the aisle and reminded me that he was holding the merchandise for me.

If your new acquisitions are too big to carry back home in your luggage, selecting a *transiteur*, or shipper, becomes an essential part of the Puces experience. In fact these agents can do much more than ship—they will pay for and pick up the merchandise, pack the goods, ship, insure, clear customs and deliver to your home. Having the *transiteur* pay for the merchandise saves you the trouble of having cash in hand when you shop, and it enables you to be comfortable that you will get what you chose. This is especially helpful in the case of repairs. If there is an agreed-upon repair, the shipper can verify that it has been properly carried out before the merchandise is paid for and leaves the stand. This can make the difference between a success and a nightmare, but in shipping, as in everything else, you get what you pay for. There are many war stories of badly packed merchandise, uninsured purchases, pieces arriving in different condition than purchased, and so on. The shippers have booths at the Puces. If you know in advance that you will need one, it is best to introduce yourself at the start of your quest. The shipper will arm you with purchase orders, stickers and tags to properly identify your purchases. Carry a digital camera to help you remember the pieces you bought and their condition at the time of purchase.

The best way to learn about the Puces is to experience it in small doses. Listen, look, experience the feelings. Put on a big smile and a friendly attitude. It will make your experience positive, enlightening, and enjoyable. Above all, don't be discouraged if you don't immediately find that one special thing, and be willing to be surprised and captivated by the unexpected treasure.

LEFT
Typical objects that can be found at the Marché aux Puces. On the wall is a copper "fontaine" or washing vessel. The candelabra is turned walnut. The box in tooled leather is in unusually good condition for a flea market find.

OPPOSITE
A symmetrical arrangement of gilt metal sconces flanks an octagonal mirror. Candlestick bouillotte lamps flank an eighteenth-century clock.

This handsome bedroom is filled with flea market finds: the armoire, the headboard, the eighteenth-century commode. the lamps, and even the painting.

LEFT

*Unusual is what to look for the in the Marché aux
Puces. The tiny semannier, the cane chair, the Louis
Vuitton chest are all objects that make a room unique.*

ABOVE

*A country French cabinet from the Marché Biron fits
the color scheme perfectly.*

OPPOSITE
*A spectacular mirrored dressing table from
the 1930s from the Marché aux Puces.*

RIGHT
*This lovely screeen is the type of object
to design a room around.*

Collecting

ollecting is a human instinct. For as long as people have focused on acquiring more objects than they needed, they have turned that excess into collections, automatically, instinctively. A collection can be a simple grouping of mugs or an elaborate presentation of rare, ancient artifacts.

In France, collecting has its own vocabulary, starting with the simplest *chiner*, to bargain-hunt, to the more descriptive, *farfouiller*, *brocanter* and *collecter*, to collect. A *brocanteur* typically is a bric-à-brac seller, and *brocante* itself, to be plain, is collectible junk. There is, in fact, a difference between a *brocante* market and an antique market, although there always seems to be a bit of each in both.

In the countryside of France, in the most modest inns, there are often collections of cuisine-related items, such as coffeepots, coffee grinders, and copper pots. The collections in stately homes or house museums, such as the Jacquemart-André and the Musée Camondo, are wide-ranging, including everything from curios to boxes, furniture and tapestries, paintings, and decorative works of art. Country châteaux convey life as it was for the upper classes; their tastes and interests are reflected in their collections. In the dining rooms, for example, the china and crystal collections are almost infinite, with dishes designed for every culinary morsel—the nut dish, the pickle dish, the dried fruit server, or *fruit-sec*. These were not hidden, as they might be today. Instead they were and still are displayed in large and lovely china rooms. Curiously, the abundance of china and crystal contrasts with the absence of silver. The troubled times of the late eighteenth century forced Louis XVI to melt down silver, and much of the silver displayed today is nineteenth century or later.

Parisian homes are filled with collections. The French love to collect, acquiring both at permanent markets, such as the Marché aux Puces and the Louvre des Antiquaires, Village Suisse, and the rue St. Paul area in the Marais in Paris or at any number of weekly and annual fairs, held both in Paris and in the provinces. In addition there are street fairs and ad hoc *marchés* in Paris and all over the country on a weekly basis. Perhaps the best

known of these are the markets in Isle sur la Sorgue and the biannual fair in Toulouse. The magazine *Aladin* lists the fairs and shows around the country by date and place.

Displaying collections adds to the pleasure of acquiring them. To the collector, each item in the collection has a meaning, a story. There is the tale of the conquest and the story of its origins. The size of the objects determines how they might be displayed. Small objects, such as inkwells, paperweights, or perfume bottles can be grouped together on an end table or coffee table, where they can be easily admired. Larger pieces—tea caddies or porcelain figures, for example—may need a large table, bookcase, or *étagère*. Sculptures, depending on their size, can be come a focal point in a room. Flat objects, such as antique fans, look best grouped together, framed individually or in multiples.

In the process of collecting, collectors become immersed in their subject, training their eye by examining the objects, soliciting advice from dealers, and consulting relevant books, auction catalogs, and periodicals. Knowing the range of the field and following the market enables the collector to discuss potential purchases intelligently and negotiate successfully. Whatever the collecting area, the vendor knows it well, both in terms of what the objects can fetch in the marketplace and how to judge quality. Tortoise boxes are typically English, but they are acquired across the Channel by many collectors. Their look is also very chic and they are at home in almost any setting and therefore sought after. There are, of course, specialists who collect and resell them *en masse*. Although this is an easy way of creating an instant collection, true collectors snub their noses at this method. It takes away the fun, and one pays an enormous premium.

Auction houses are an important resource for collectors. The most famous—Sotheby's and Christie's—are international with offices in New York and London and throughout Europe and Asia. There are many smaller local auction houses throughout the United States, and their catalogs are accessible online. In France, Tajan is a wonderful auctioneer, and the catalogs are available by subscription.

When in Paris, pick up a magazine called *Gazette de l'Hôtel Drouot*, which lists all the auctions taking place that week. Drouot, a world unto itself, is located in the 9th arronidissement. Auction items are either on display or auctions are taking place in each of its sixteen rooms, often with several auctions taking place at the same time under the auspices of different auctioneers. Drouot provides exhibition and auction rooms for one hundred auctioneers, some with elaborate catalogs and others with minimal, unillustrated lists. Drouot is a place that must be visited to be comprehended. The exhibition rooms, which often seem to be piled with junk, must be seen in person to know if a prospective treasure is really a treasure or another forgettable facsimile. The pace is very fast and it's easy to be moved by the heat of the moment. Nevertheless, Drouot is well worth a visit.

Parisians collect with passion. Antique flea markets, fairs and shows are held all over the country and in many small villages, antique *marchés*, or *brocantes* are fixed, weekly affairs. Thus the collections grow easily. Parisians display their collections in varying ways, but organized clutter seems to be the rule. This is one instance in Parisian décor where more can be more. Small *bibelots* and *objets* can cover every surface of the Parisian home. It may be that reproducing this look is as elusive as tying that proverbial scarf, but it can be fun to try. Collections are, above all, personal. They are the individuality added to a room. Collections add warmth, charm, and that *je ne sais quoi* to one's home. It may seem difficult to get started, but once the search has begun, it can be rewarding in many ways.

*End tables flanking
a sofa are not a pair
but they are
balanced with small
collections—iron
tazzas or cassolettes
on the left and a
group of Régule
urns on the right.*

OVERLEAF
*This intricate
bronze desk set is
signed Tiffany, but it
was found in Paris.*

A collection of blue and white earthen ware in a buffet en deux corps.

A group of tortoiseshell boxes and a turned wood lamp

ABOVE
*Antique seals, mounted on black velvet and
framed, hang with a print by Miro.*

OPPOSITE
*A bar embellished with Victorian-era ice buckets
in both silver and crystal and oak trimmed in
silver. The old wine jugs add a whimsical touch.*

OPPOSITE
An eclectic grouping: a terrestrial globe, marble vases, rare shell on stand and iron, and old French wooden games standing on a wooden box.

RIGHT
Two Lalique perfume bottles, glass objects, and golden glass perfume bottles displayed on an étagère with hints of Chinoiserie.

A very French grouping of objects and flowers united by a single color.

A collection of seals framed and arranged symmetrically.

ABOVE LEFT
A silver tea set and candlesticks displayed in an informal pantry setting.

ABOVE RIGHT
French ceramic canisters in blue and white pick up the color of the tiles behind them.

OPPOSITE
Earthenware pots add charm to this kitchen buffet

LEFT
Rectangular putti in gilded frames
repeat the squares of the fabric
and wall covering.

OPPOSITE
A grouping of bull's eye mirrors
above a dressing bable.

Sources

Paint

Farrow and Ball
112 Mercer Street, New York
50 Rue de l'Université, Paris

Ressource
4 Avenue du Maine, Paris

Antiques

Antiques on Old Park Road
Westmont, Illinois

Mike Bell
1869 Merchandise Mart, Chicago

Le Douze
12 Rue Jacob, Paris

Sylvain Levy-Alban
14 Rue de Beaune, Paris

Nicole Mugler
2 Rue de l'Université, Paris

Galerie Altero
21 Quai Voltaire, Paris

Tajan Auctions
37 Rue des Mathurins, Paris

Hôtel Drouot
9 Rue Drouot, Paris

Lee Calicchio
306 East 61st Street, New York

Amy Perlin
306 East 61st Street, New York

Sentimento
306 East 61st Street, New York

Sotheby's
1334 York Avenue, New York
76 Rue du Faubourg Saint Honoré, Paris

Christie's
20 Rockefeller Plaza, New York
9 Avenue Matignon Paris

Lighting

Galerie des Lampes
9 Rue de Beaune, Paris

Delisle, Paris
4 Rue du Parc-Royal, Paris

Carlos de la Puente
238 East 60th Street, New York

Nicholas Antiques
979 Third Avenue, New York

Fireplaces

Vieilles Pierres du Mellois
101 Rue des Rosiers, Saint Ouen, France

Danny Alessandro
308 East 59th Street, New York 10022

Saint Ouen Flea Markets

Le Monde de Voyage
Marché Serpette
Stand 15, Allée 3

Du Billiard au Comptoir
Marché Serpette
Stand 9, Allée 4

Giles Deriot
Marché Serpette
Stand 37, Allée 1

Maison James
Marché Serpette
Stand 00, Allée 0

D'Ythurbe
Marché Serpette
Stand 25, Allee 6

S.A.D.
Marché Paul-Bert

Bachelier Antiquités
Marché Paul-Bert
Stand 17, Allée 1

Architecture and Moldings

Hyde Park Mouldings
110 Kennedy Drive, Hauppauge, New York

Design Laboratories (Architects)
31 Union Square, New York

Exquisite Surfaces (Flooring)
150 East 58th Street, New York
11 East Putnam Avenue, Greenwich, Connecticut

Furniture

Conil
1 Rue de Varenne, Paris

Sentou Galerie
26 Boulevard Raspail, Paris

Christian Liaigre
42 Rue du Bac, Paris

Mise en Demeure
27 Rue du Cherche-Midi, Paris

Catherine Memmi
11 Rue Saint Sulpice, Paris

Tabletop

Zero One One
2 Rue de Marengo, Paris

Le Bon Marché
24 Rue de Sevres, Paris

Diners en Ville
27 Rue de Varenne, Paris

Puiforcat
48 Avenue Gabriel, Paris

Bernardaud
99 Rue Rivoli, Paris
499 Park Avenue, New York

Michael C. Fina
545 Fifth Avenue, New York

Scully & Scully
504 Park Avenue, New York

Mary Mahoney
351 Worth Avenue, Palm Beach, Florida

Bergdorf Goodman
754 Fifth Avenue, New York

William Wayne
850 Lexington Avenue, New York

With many thanks to so many people who make my decorating and Parisian life possible:

Interior design support: Irwin Weiner, David Ruff, Charles Cohen, John and Steven Stark, Cydonia Boonshaft, Irene Parcells, Rona Goodman, Walters Kunzel, Sr and Jr., Jean-Charles Mouniere, Zale Contracting, Gayle Rosenberg, Regis Aernauts, Nicholas Sergeeff, Sylvain Levy-Alban, Monique Conil, and Ed Wozniac (my parents' decorator!)

Bringing Paris Home: Andrea Monfried, Elizabeth White, Stacee Lawrence, Abigail Sturges, Karen Gantz, Emma Segre Edelson, and Nina Bauer. Thank you to photographers: Kim Sargent, Francis Hammond, Marco Ricco, and Durston Saylor.

Close friends who encouraged me from the beginning: Linda Berley, Gail Nussbaum Kaplan, Andrea Stark, Harold Bernard, Gilda Ross, Barbara Annis, Joan Mantel, Lola Ryan, Michelle Friezo, Marcia Lustgarten, Holly Brown, Narfe Suico, and Barbara Solomon. My boys: Adam Baird Alpert, James Deutsch, Arie Deutsch, Alex Baird Deutsch, Benjamin Baird Deutsch, and Philip Baird Deutsch, who sometimes have to put up with the crankiest designer in history. And my parents: Philip and Terri Baird, who trained me from birth.

The journalists who have translated my work into words: Wendy Moonan, Penelope Rowlands, Stephen Drucker, Stephen Stillman, Jorge Arango, Chris Maddon, Adele Cygelman, et al and illustrator Florine Asch.

A special thanks to *Architectural Digest*, the greatest support team in the world.

Photography Credits

Numbers refer to page numbers.

Bruce Buck: 74

Ruth Cincotti/Palm Beach Life: 108, 112 (top)

Carlos Domenech: 86–87, 97, 106, 107, 110, 111, 158

Jon Elliott: 154

Francis Hammond: 1, 2–3, 6–7, 9, 10, 12–13, 14, 15, 16, 17, 18, 19, 42–43, 44, 45 48, 50, 51, 65, 68–69, 70 (left), 71 (bottom left), 73, 80, 81, 85, 88, 89, 90, 91 (top left), 93, 94, 95, 114–115, 116, 117, 118, 119, 120, 144–145, 146, 147, 149, 150, 151, 164–165, 166, 167, 168, 169, 170, 171, 172, 173, 182–183, 184–185, 187, 188, 189, 198

Frances Janisch: 160, 163

Barbel Miebach: 32, 33, 103

Marco Ricca: 28–29, 30, 38, 39, 40, 41, 49, 52–53, 54, 55, 58–59, 61, 71 (top left), 76, 77, 82, 83, 91 (bottom left), 100–101, 102, 105, 109, 123, 124–125, 131, 132–133, 134, 135, 136, 137, 157, 159, 162, 174, 175, 176, 177, 180, 190, 191, 192–193, 194, 195, 197, 199, 200, 201, 202, 203, 204, 205

Nikolas Sargent: 75, 121, 122, 139, 181

Kim Sargent: 11, 21, 22–23, 70, 71, 84, 178

Durston Saylor: 20, 24, 25, 26, 27, 31, 34–35, 36, 37, 46, 56–57, 60, 62–63, 64, 66, 67, 78–79, 91 (right), 96, 98–99, 104, 112 (bottom), 113, 126, 127, 128–129, 130, 138, 140, 141, 142–143, 152, 153, 155, 156, 161, 179, 196